THIS BOOK WILL TEACH YOU HOW TO WRITE BETTER

This book is:
Short. Effective. And sort of offensive.
But you will write better after reading this.

"Communication is just getting information from one brain, to another brain."

Learn how to **get what you want.**
Learn how to **increase your conversion rates.**
Learn how to **make it easier to write anything** (using formulas and mind-hacks).

by: Neville N. Medhora

CONTENTS OF THIS BOOK:

HI THERE!

Dammit. I wanted to make this book long. But I'm gonna limit it to less than 100 pages.
Why? Because I have a short attention span too.

But don't be fooled. **Brevity does not equal cheapness.**

Only fools believe something must be long to be valuable. The information inside has turned keystrokes from my fingers, into millions of dollars in sales.

Some of the concepts inside have been able to turn a poor man, into a rich man, by simply re-arranging some words on a page.

Like nuclear secrets, this information can be used for good, or for evil.

Someone can take this information and bring in millions of dollars for a charity.

Someone can take this information and spread their awesome products to the world.

Someone can also take this information and scam people into buying a shitty product.

Watch out for that last one. Karma's a bitch.
It's SO much easier to make money the legit way. So let's stay there.

While this booky-book is shorty-short, tt should also swell your head with ideas, making the read-time much longer.

I hope you have a notepad ready.
I hope you have a pen ready.
I hope you have a tasty beverage in hand (a nice beer, whiskey, or tea will suffice).

Because we're about to get started.
Giddyup!

Ch. 1
THE ENVELOPE EXERCISE

Let's take two envelopes. Each has a postal stamp on it.

Let's take two pieces of paper. Both of them are completely blank.

Let's address them. Both of them....to your mother.

So now we've got two envelopes, both addressed to your mom, both almost ready to send.

In the first envelope, let's write a letter to dear old momma:

> Hey mom!
>
>
> I'm writing this letter to let you know that while I haven't called you in awhile, I think about you everyday, and how fortunate I am to have a mom like you!
>
> No matter what I do, where I go, and how much I've messed up, you've always been there supporting me....and I can't tell you how much that means to me.
>
> Sometimes I hear friends complain about their moms, but I can't do the same. I've always appreciated how well you've taken care of me, and as I get older and understand more about the hardships of life, I respect you EVEN MORE with every passing year.
>
> So this is just a short reminder, to let you know, that I love you so incredibly much....and feel blessed to have such a great mom!
>
> Love you!
> -Johnny McFakename

Awwww.....now isn't that sweet?

Let's fold that letter up, and seal it inside envelope number one.

Ok....now let's write another letter!

Hello my "so-called" mother,

I'd like to drop you a short note, letting you know that every living day I've spent with you has been a miserable hell.

I feel that everything you say, do, and teach me has been a curse on my life. The best part of my life was when I moved away from you.

I am envious of all my friends who have REAL mothers, and saddened that I was given you as my mother. If I had a say in it, I would have never selected such a poor choice of mother.

In fact, I tell my friends I don't even have a mother, because in my mind you were never fit to be one.

I'd like to end this note by saying:
I hope I never see your horrible face and personality again in my life.

Screw off and DIE.
Hatefully,
-Johnny McFakename

P.S. Dad sucks too.

Ok....now let's fold this letter up and stuff it inside envelope number two.

NOW....
What do you think would happen if we mailed the nice letter?
We might get a smiley mother who loves us even more and has warmed heart.

What do you think would happen if we mailed the not-so-nice letter? We'd have a crying mother who hates us, feels horrible about herself, and would be rocked to her very core to read that letter.

The ONLY difference between those two letters, was simply:
The words on the page.

Same stamps.
Same address.
Same envelopes.

I want you to remember this:
The words on a page, can have an ENORMOUS impact on someone else.

If you learn this fact well, it can help you make a lot more money, and help get what you want.

This is a famous example the copywriter Gary Halbert would give during conferences, and it demonstrates this PERFECTLY.

Just remember: Words can have a HUGE impact on your conversions, of anything.

Ch. 2
No one cares about you

Awww man, this is gonna hurt....

Nobody cares about you. They only care about themselves.

Got that?

People don't care about **YOU**.
They care about **THEMSELVES.**

I want you to repeat that in your head three times
(out loud please):

"No one cares about me, they care about themselves..."
"No one cares about me, they care about themselves....."
"No one cares about me, they care about themselves......."

So why are we repeating this depressing statement? Well it's
simple:

When people come to something new, they immediately assess
if it's USEFUL to them.

So if a pregnant woman stumbles upon a page called:
"How to avoid stretch marks when you're pregnant"

.....she'll likely be very interested. She'll probably never know
the name of the person who wrote the article, however the
information applies directly to her!

THIS IS A VERY POWERFUL CONCEPT MY YOUNG
APPRENTICE.
REMEMBER IT.

When people come across the things you write, you immediately want to get their attention by at least implying **what it can do for them.**

Waaayy too many websites/emails/letters incessantly talk about themselves first. Kind of like:

> Welcome to Ace Tennis Coaching. We are dedicated to serving our customers. We have been focusing on quality service for years, and have a dedicated staff to help fulfill your tennis needs. Our team is focused on quality coaching and delivering great training. We aim to serve our customers needs blah BLah BLAH.

Did you get ANYTHING out of this fluff writing?
NO!!

It was all about THEM, and nothing about YOU.
If you're a greedy little monkey like I am, then you're more interested in what the company can do for YOU.

Maybe something like this would grab people a little more:

Every amateur tennis player has the exact same problem with their tennis swing:

They don't bend their elbow at the proper angle for their height.

Sounds really simple, but we see it every day....chances are you bend your elbow incorrectly also, and we're going to show you how to hit the ball harder simply by changing the bend of your elbow.

This little body-hack will let you:
- Hit the ball harder, without swinging harder.
- Hit the "sweet spot" of the ball with each swing.
- Increase the speed of your serve by 20%.

All these improvements come from simply bending your

---

elbow in a slightly different position!

This is just the first thing we teach you at Ace Tennis Coaching. Our more advanced training will improve your game beyond what you thought possible.

Our professional coaches have helped over 800 people like you take their tennis game from amateur to professional.

We'll spot all the small things you're doing wrong, and work with you individually to correct them and crush your competition.

Come by for an analysis of how you can improve your tennis swing. It only takes 20 minutes, and we'll identify all the tweaks you can make in your game which will take you to the next level.

See? We talked about the company a little, but the main point was the benefit the customer would get.

THIS is what the customer is interested in!!!
We only mentioned something "about us" to establish some trust and credibility.

So remember that phrase we repeated in the beginning?
Here it is again:

People don't care about us, they care about themselves.

Through this frame of mind, we can better assist people, and better get people to read our stuff. For example, you can describe everything a person is interested in, in one small title:
- "How to avoid getting stretch marks"
- "Three ways to increase email opt-ins"
- "Why the Tyrannosaurus Rex has such short arms"

All of those titles directly describe what's about to happen in that article.

People interested in the article will stay, and the ones not interested will leave.

BONUS:
We can even sex-up those titles by <u>adding more descriptive images in the persons head:</u>
- "How to avoid gross stretch marks on your belly"
- "Three ways to increase email opt-ins before your lunch break is over"
- "Why does the Tyrannosaurus Rex have hilariously short arms?"

I want you to basically remember to LET PEOPLE KNOW WHAT BENEFIT THEY'RE GONNA GET!

Ch. 3
Write funny.
Write informative.
Just not boring.

My dear student.....how often have you said to your sweetie, "Baby....let's go out tonight to that really boring restaurant, with the incredibly mediocre food, and then see that movie that we heard was reallyyyy boring."

Never ever ever.

If you want people to listen to what you have to say, you need to be interesting!

Even if you have something interesting to say, your delivery can make people read, or run.

Lemme give you an example:
Have you ever had a high school or college teacher that was REALLY BORING?

Something about them just put you to sleep. Even though they're technically teaching you exactly what you need to know, the material just didn't absorb into your head because of the way they presented it.

Now, have you ever had a high school or college teacher that was REALLY AWESOME?

Even if it was a class about boring material, there was something about the teacher that kept you engaged and in your seat WANTING to listen.

I'd venture to guess you'd rather take a class by an interesting professor?
Duh.

Likewise, people enjoy reading INTERESTING articles, that are also WELL WRITTEN.

This is actually a shockingly easy task to do, and I'm going to reveal how...right now on the next page:

Write
casual copy!

....that's it.
That's the whole secret!

And when I say "Casual Copy", I mean write in a style that's casual to you.

Imagine you're in a booth, at a diner, with a close friend, eating lunch.

Explain to him what you're trying to sell, without boring him.

Let's pretend you sell something "boring" like enterprise-grade computer systems.

While having lunch, would you say to your friend:

> ::(in a nerdy, monotonous voice)::
> "Dear friend, I would like to extend my services to you to explain to you the benefits of the P-800 enterprise grade computer system. We are proud to offer this as our flagship product of Oxford Computer Systems. Our P-800 is a high tech solution for common needs amongst enterprise clients."

....of course you would never speak to him like that.

If you spoke like this, by now your friend would be looking for rope to make a noose and kill himself!

So if you'd never speak like that, WHY WOULD YOU WRITE LIKE THAT??!?

We're all guilty of sitting down to type, then getting stiff and bland in our writing, especially in the corporate world.

We're all somehow taught this from a young age. I'm going to try and break you out of that habit.

Why?
Because when people start writing more "Casual Copy", I've seen their responses/sales/engagement go up upwards of 10x....simply from changing the words they use.

So let's try to un-boring-ify what we told our friend about the computer systems we sell:

> "So you know how when you go through a toll road it takes a photo of your license plate? Well storing that huge photo, decoding what it says, looking up that license number in a database of millions of drivers, then billing your account....takes A LLOOTT of computer power.
>
> The system we sell can process over 50 cars per second, but our closest competitor sells a system that costs twice as much, and does only 10 cars per second. So in heavy traffic, 30% of revenue is lost because the computer can't keep up.
>
> Basically.... our P-800 computer system:
> - Costs half as much as our competition.
> - Processes 5x as much information.
> - ....and immediately makes 30% more revenue for our clients.
>
> And that's just toll roads! NASA actually saves a million bucks a month using our system for their shuttle program......but I won't bore you, I'll tell you that story another time!"

Holy crap!! I'm not looking to buy an enterprise computer system, but THAT one sounds damn cool after those examples! And the way we ended it, makes the other person ANXIOUS TO KNOW MORE!

So in conclusion:
The 1st "boring" example: Leaves the person wanting to kill themselves, and hoping you shut up.

The 2nd "casual copy" example: Leaves the person with a clear understanding of what the computer system can do, the very-obvious advantages of your product, and leaves them wanting more information.

I'd say "writing casually" can have a pretty damn great effect on whatever you're trying to sell.

"Ok ok ok Neville.....I get it, you're awesome at writing copy. But I can't do that!"

Oh yea? Try these simple steps to make your copy more casual:

1. Grab your phone, or anything to record your voice. Start recording.
2. Pretend you're in that same booth having dinner with your friend.
3. In your own words, between friends, explain to him why what you're selling is so amazing.
4. Stop recording, and transcribe exactly what you wrote. Err's and Umm's included.

BOOM. What you wrote is probably already a lot more clear than generic-boring-copy.

You can take-n-grab the parts that sound interesting, and cut the parts that are boring.

Simply slapping this transcription together is often MUCH BETTER THAN PROFESSIONALLY WRITTEN (yet boring) COPY!

It's really that simple.

We'll go further into some actual tactics you can use, but remember that casual copy is often the most engaging.

Ch. 4
Ohh wait....
....don't write TOO wacky

Ok, the last chapter told you to "write like you speak."

I'm guessing your speech is somewhere between boring, and talking like a clown. So:

(BORING SNOOZE-FEST) ---(YOU ARE HERE)--- (TALKING LIKE A DRUNK CLOWN)

In my experience, sometimes people take this "casual copy" advice to the absolute edge, to where they just sound plain wacky & weird.

Don't do this.

Remember: The point of your copy is to get the reader to take action. Don't use jokes SO often that they distract from the main message.

Casual Copy does NOT have to always be humorous. It just has to be "real."

A friend wanted me to help out a startup he invested in, so I wrote some copy for an email they were sending out (it was a site that sold deals for nightlife in Hollywood).

They HATED the first email I sent to them, but after some convincing, they ran with it. It converted 65% better than their best performing email.

They shut the hell up after they saw those dollar signs.

But after they tried to lower my contracting price, I refused to do anything else with them, and they attempted to copy my style themselves.

A week later they sent out this email snippet to their entire customer base:

> As everyone knows, Hollywood is famous for class, high fashion, and brilliantly beautiful art. This is truer today than ever before. Also, I just bought a time machine and am writing this on my new Remington Portable typewriter. I'm sitting in the basement of a Los Angeles library (I'd tell you where, but I don't want to attract the fuzz) and drinking a Gloria Swanson, which seems to be some combination of dark liquor and cold, stale coffee, and is named for the starlet who frequents the joint. Prohibition has really.....[link to website]

After all that writing....do you still have ANY idea what they're trying to sell??

It went on like that for 4 paragraphs, and even continued their "jokes" into the selling. I couldn't follow along without being confused.

They tried to "write wacky", but it totally backfired. The email did awfully, people unsubscribed, and till this day I still don't know what the hell that email was trying to sell.

They tried to use SO MUCH HUMOR that it became **useless & annoying**.

And if an email is **useless & annoying**....it's called SPAM and I unsubscribe from it.

Don't forget the point of writing better is not to be a silly jackass...it's to SELL SELL SELL.

Stop trying to be clever. Instead be CLEAR.

If you ever think something you just wrote is TOO WACKY...here's a question to ask:

"IS THIS ADDING TO THE USERS KNOWLEDGE??"

"AM I HELPING THEM GET THROUGH THIS BY ADDING THIS IN?"

If it DOES help make your writing more interesting and still sell them...then leave it in.

If it's DISTRACTING to the reader.....Take it out.

Be ruthless about axing copy that confuses people.

TIPS:
- If you're TOO proud of a joke or sentence you wrote, it's probably too complicated. Take it out.
- If something you wrote is "meh"....delete it immediately. Don't leave it on the page.
- The point of your copy is to get the reader to take action.
- Don't ever lose their attention, or they stop reading.

Ch. 5
People respond to what is New, Novel, or Helpful.

Normally you can't force people to read something or consume something. So you must make it so that they WANT to pay attention.

Here's some things people pay attention to:

People pay attention to what is <u>new</u>.
If someone passes the same road every day, they might never pay attention to the billboards, unless they consciously notice a NEW one.

People pay attention to what is <u>novel</u>.
You might not pay attention to what people are wearing, but you sure will notice a guy walking around with a "HONK IF YOU FARTED" t-shirt wouldn't you? The novelty caught your attention.

People pay attention to what is <u>helpful</u>.
If you're growing an awesome beard, and you're going through a magazine, and an article says, **"3 ways to make your awesome beard more awesome-er"**, that would be helpful information to you.

So those are three of the main ways we can capture people's attention, but there's a limit to some of these:

NEW: Being "new" wears off quickly. Can't always depend on this.

NOVEL: You can dress like a clown at a business conference which will get you attention, but it might not give you the RIGHT attention. Attention is good, but <u>only if it results in buyers</u>.

HELPFUL: Now here's a useful tactic. BEING HELPFUL!!
If you're helpful to people, they'll WANT to listen to you, they'll WANT to subscribe to you, and they'll WANT to pay for your services.

I'd say that "being helpful" seems to be a pretty damn great way to get attention, eh!

You see "How To" articles all over the place, and the reason is those articles tell people how to solve a problem.

Simple.

SO if you help people solve problems, they will pay attention.

This is a key component to what made my writing different from everyone else. I spouted useful information, but also sold at the same time.

So even if someone doesn't want to buy the thing I'm selling, they will STILL learn something useful from the sales email/letter/website/mail.

This way they stay tuned in to EVERYTHING I write.

Use this principle for your:
- Emails
- Webpages
- Videos
- ...everything.

MAKE IT HELPFUL, THEY WILL LISTEN.

Ch. 6
The All-important AIDA formula.

Look.

There's no RIGHT way to write.
If you write something, and the other person "gets its".....then you've succeeded.

HOWEVER, there are ways which have been proven to be <u>more efficient</u> at selling than <u>others</u>. This formula is one of them.

<u>A quick personal note about this formula that I'm gonna teach you:</u>
The day I learned this formula, I stayed up till 6am thinking about how EVERY SINGLE THING I've ever sold up till that point, was damn-near wrong compared to this.

I thought about products I sold online, sales pitches I did door-to-door, and even emails where I was trying to get something. All would have been GREATLY IMPROVED if I just knew this simple framework first.

From that day forward when I started applying this principle, I started making more money, I started getting more recognition for my writing, and I was able to get more of what I wanted.

It was simple as applying this 4-letter formula to anything I communicated.

So listen up Bob, this could change your life!
(Sorry for calling you Bob).....

The formula goes like this:

A.I.D.A.

It stands for:

Attention
Interest
Desire
Action

Repeat that with me. Maybe make a song or jingle out of it to remember it better:
Attention, **I**nterest, **D**esire, **A**ction.

Here's how you use this formula:
Use this formula when writing to someone (if it's a group of people, pretend it's just ONE person).

You first get their **ATTENTION**.
This will get them to at least read what you have to say.

You then capture their **INTEREST**.
You have their attention already, now get them to slide deeper down the slope by getting them genuinely interested in what you've gotta say. Tell them interesting facts and interesting things it can do.

You make them **DESIRE** your product.
By now you should have made them under-their-own-will WANT to either buy your product, or take whatever action you want them to. Show them what life could be with this. Tell them how much faster a problem would be solved with this. Show them how someone's life was greatly improved by it, and how they can have the same results.

You make them take an **ACTION**.
Get them to go and buy it! Or click a link. Or take whatever step you want them to.

Describe how to do that action, and tell them what will happen after they do it. Hold them by the hand and describe how everything will work.

I can do an entire course about this formula, but I wanna install this knowledge in your head FAST, so let's jump to some examples:

From my **www.KopywritingKourse.com** website I took this template.

Use this general template as a guide to start writing your sales message. Simply fill this out and you're pretty much done with the whole sales message.

(I personally write at least 4 titles before settling on one subject line or headline):

Subject line 1: Sample subject email line
Subject line 2: Sample subject email line
Subject line 3: Sample subject email line
Subject line 4: Sample subject email line

<u>ATTENTION</u>: grab their attention in this section.
text text text

<u>INTEREST</u>: Interest them with interesting facts about it.
text text text

<u>DESIRE</u>: Make them desire the product or action to take.
text text text

<u>**ACTION**</u>**: Describe to them exactly HOW they should take action, and when they should do it by.**
text text text

Link to Checkout the Thingamabob Here →
Sincerely,
Your name

P.S. A friendly reminder to hurry up and do the action.

Let's fill out some quick examples using this template:
Maybe try these out on your own too….. just jot them down in a
notebook on some throw-away paper.

Goal:
Convince Jason to buy a helicopter.

Subject 1: Every CEO has a helicopter, why don't you?
Subject 2: Hate traffic on I-35 in the morning? Drive OVER it
Subject 3: How to save 300 hours per year of frustration
Subject 4: Own a helicopter and: Make more, drive less, be happier

<u>**ATTENTION**</u>**: grab their attention in this section.**
Hey Jason,

You know how that drive from your apartment to the office is SO brutal that you end up cursing at everyone who cuts in front of you? Well if you had a helicopter, that wouldn't even be an issue!

INTEREST: Interest them with interesting facts about it.
With a helicopter, you would:

- ...get to work in only 20% of the time.
- ...have no more frustration when you get to work.
- ...have a fun ride to anywhere in your city within minutes.
- ...not have to live by the rules "normal" people do!

DESIRE: Make them desire the product or action to take.
Your time is worth about $200/hour, and since you spend an average of 300 extra hours in traffic each year, you're losing out on $60,000 in income!!!

Not to mention that after all that frustrating traffic, work is the LAST thing you want to do.

That's why having a helicopter would make your life so much more enjoyable, and even help you make more money.

ACTION: Describe to them exactly HOW they should take action, and when they should do it.
I have 3 people looking to sell their helicopters now, and wanna show them to you. When can I send you the specs and prices of these helicopters?

Also, if you'd like to call me, just pick up the phone and dial 713.301.1546 and I'll answer any questions you have.

Sincerely,
Your name

P.S. The CEO of Ardent Labs here in town has a helicopter, and said it was the #1 thing that made him want to come to work each morning!

Goal:
Convince someone it's worth it to live.

Subject 1: Life sucks right? Not really, here's some easy changes...
Subject 2: A few simple steps you can take to make your life better.
Subject 3: How to reverse a shitty life
Subject 4: Make a crappy life, into a great life

<u>ATTENTION</u>: grab their attention in this section.
Sometimes life seems completely, and utterly, overwhelming. When everything sucks in your life, sometimes death seems better.

Obviously if certain things in your life were better, you'd WANT to live. Right? If so, then let's do something about changing your life around.

<u>INTEREST</u>: Interest them with interesting facts about it.
Let's break down your life into three areas:
-**Health:** Your general state of health.
-**Wealth:** Your money situation.
-**Love:** You relationships with friends, family, significant others

etc.

Rate each on a scale from 1 to 5.

Now if you're reading this, I bet most of them are pretty low. But find the lowest number.

Example:
Health: 1
Wealth: 4
Love: 2

DESIRE: **Make them desire the product or action to take.**
Find an area where you're really low, and bummed about it. Now get out a small scrap of paper (you can keep in your pocket), and list out 5 things you could do (be precise) to improve that number.

ACTION: **Describe to them exactly HOW they should take action, and when they should do it by.**
I want you to start trying the simplest of those 5 things today. And keep doing them until you fill all 5.

This might sound incredibly simple, but try it out RIGHT NOW, and see if your life doesn't start changing one day at a time.

Sincerely,
Your name

P.S. If you would like me to keep you accountable, tell me your goals for the month. Leave a message on my phone at 713.301.1546 or send me an email with your goals at NevMed@gmail.com. I will follow up with you in one month to see your progress.

Goal:
Convince someone to buy a laptop computer instead of a desktop.

Subject 1: Modern laptops are powerful as desktop computers

Subject 2: Why keep your computer in one place, when you can take it anywhere?

Subject 3: Wireless synching to big screens makes desktop computers irrelevant.

Subject 4: Unless you're editing a Hollywood movie, you don't need a desktop computer.

ATTENTION: grab their attention in this section.

If you were buying a music album 30 years ago, the newly released "Thriller" from Michael Jackson was a good bet. And if you were looking to buy a computer, a big-ole clunker would be sitting on your desk soon.

But that's changed a WHOLE lot. Now a laptop computer like the MacBook Air has so much computing power inside, it makes no sense to buy a desktop computer.

INTEREST: Interest them with interesting facts about it.

Since 2004 desktop computer sales have fell 15% each year, because NO ONE NEEDS THAT MUCH COMPUTING POWER ANYMORE!

Even video makers have whole home studios based off one MacBook laptop computer.

Now only high-end graphics designers and videographers need the computer horsepower of a desktop computer.

DESIRE: Make them desire the product or action to take.
Even the cheapest laptop on the market is like a mini super-computer compared to the technology of just 10 years ago.

So if you're looking to do email, write documents, make some videos, listen to music and other "normal" stuff on a computer, I can recommend this ONE thing:

ACTION: Describe to them exactly HOW they should take action, and when they should do it by.
JUST....GET....A....LAPTOP!

You'll thank me later!

Sincerely,
Neville Medhora - Computer geek

P.S. I'm typing these words from a 0.6 inch MacBook Air laptop on my balcony overlooking Downtown Austin, TX.
 Can't do THAT on a desktop stuck in a room!

Ch. 7
Think about "Bob" and how you'd talk to him over coffee. Write like that.

If there's one good piece of advice I'd give you, it's KNOW YOUR MARKET.

It's best to actually **be** your market, because then you know exactly what customers want.

I'm not a golfer, so I'd be at a disadvantage if I was trying to sell golf clubs compared to someone who's REALLY into golf.

So you need to make a customer, "Bob" .

A "Bob" is a composite average customer you're trying to sell to.

So if we're trying to sell high end golf equipment, we'd be looking for avid golfers with a lot of money.

This person would probably be:
- White.
- Married.
- Have kids.
- Watches CNN.
- Business owner.
- Between 40 and 65
- Industry professional.
- He makes about 280k/year.
- Own a home near a golf course.

This is a good start for our "Bob".

So let's imagine a guy named Robert, he lives in a gated community with a golf course, has 2 kids, been married 17 years, he's 50, he's a dentist, and owns his own dental practice.

Here's Robert performing a root canal!

Now that we can envision Robert, how can we better sell to him??

Well the 1st step is to start THINKING LIKE HIM.
Imagine what his problems are.
Imagine what his goals are.
Imagine his desires.

Now we're only talking about selling golf clubs here, but this all relates. For example, since he's a business owner and a dentist, it's likely he's an A-type personality person that's really competitive.

What do competitive people want?
TO WIN.
TO BE THE BEST.
TO BEAT THEIR FRIENDS.

So with this knowledge, we can write a headline or subject line that grabs his attention like this:

"Two guys. Same skill level. But the guy with the Acme Club hits further every time."

"A solid-Tritium core in these clubs hits the ball further and straighter.....every time."

"Drive the ball 15 yards further than with your current club. Guaranteed."

Catch my drift here?
We're trying to appeal to Robert's deep desire to gain an advantage over his friends.

Robert probably doesn't care much about the deep science behind the clubs, but would rather just know it helps him hit further. We know this because we know HIM.

If we wanted to appeal to the "prestige" side of Robert, we'd write something like:

"My favorite clubs? Acme. They're the best."
---Tiger Woods.

"8 out of 10 pro circuit golfers use Acme Clubs."

So it's very important to get into the minds of the customer.

Here are some great questions to ask and swirl around in your head about who's buying your stuff:
- Male or female?
- Are they wealthy?
- How old are they?
- Do they have kids?
- What's their day like?
- What are some of their biggest fears?
- Why are they coming to YOU for help?
- What exactly can you help them with the most?

Ch. 8
Text is art. Style your stuff!

Somewhere along the way we were taught to follow every grammar rule. But why?
The only point of writing is to communicate thoughts to someone.

So if I write:
hey wat r u doin?

….even though it's not "proper English" you still understood it as much as this text:
Hey, what are you doing?

In fact, the poorly formatted and mis-spelled version got the point across with **less** effort.

Just keep in mind, "Communication is just transferring information from one brain to another."

….and however we can do that best, should win.

So to keep things interesting sometimes, we can use text as art rather than just text. Here's some tricks I use to make my text into art:

The Staggered List:

If I'm writing out a list of things, I'll make that list into "art". I'll take a random list like:

Things I want my website to do:
- Show off my best articles.
- Get more clients.
- Answer some commonly asked questions about my consulting business.
- Teach people about me.
- Sell my products at all times of the day.
- Rank in the search engines.

That list is ok.....but I'd personally "make it into art" to keep the reader engaged, and scrolling down that list with the least amount of brain power. Like this:

Things I want my website to do:
- Get more clients.
- Teach people about me.
- Show off my best articles.
- Rank in the search engines.
- Sell my products at all times of the day.
- Answer some commonly asked questions about my consulting business.

See how that "gentle slope" the text creates just keeps you going down the list till you're done?

Bolding:

Wanna emphasize something? I'd suggest simply bolding it. Like this:

If you're participating in The Running of the Bulls in Spain, I'd highly encourage you **not to wear red!**

Try not to do it too much. Maybe once every paragraph.

However there's no offical rule to this. If it helps communication, use it when needed.

Centering:

If you're writing something with a big build-up, a nice "center" does quite nicely. This even works well with quotes. It goes something like this:

Now I'm about to reveal a mindset shift I had, which completely changed my business life.

Once I learned this trick, everything I wrote got a better response, was shared more, and sold more. It was so damn simple I sincerely wish I'd discovered it ten years earlier.

You too can keep this simple sentence in your head, and it will change the way you ask for things, write things, and do business.

This mindset is as follows:

"No one cares about YOU, they care about THEMSELVES!"

Remember and internalize that sentence, and it will change the way you write.

See how I created a build-up and then a dramatic introduction? Kind of like a magician pulling the cloth off a cage to reveal the woman has disappeared:

build up...
Build Up......
BUild UP..........
BUILd UP...............
BUILD UP.......................

------ BIG REVEAL!! ------

Using punctuation & capitalization as art:

Oh wow.....I just showed you another one of my "text as art" techniques right before this!

See how I used those periods to create buildup?

See how I used upper-casing select letters to create the "getting bigger" effect?

Use punctuation how you want to.

There used to be someone who would edit my copy that always got on my case that "a proper ellipsis is only three periods long. Not four. Not five."

I one day got fed up and told her:
"Here's how much product awesome copy has sold: **A LOT.**
Here's how much product proper ellipsis etiquette has sold:
ZERO."

Fonts and Sizing:

I prefer whatever is easiest to read....and usually that's plain-old boring fonts like Arial and Times New Roman.

I'm a huge fan of Arial sized 12.
It's easy to read and all devices recognize it.

Black text, on white background is best for lots of reading.

Ch. 9
Subject Lines

In the A.I.D.A. chapter I showed you the blank template I write with. And you may have noticed 4 subject lines per piece of copy.

This is to help jog the ole brain and get some good ideas flowing.

A good subject or header can GRAB people's attention.
If you never grab someone's attention, they'll never read your article.

Here's a formula you can use:

Easy headline formula:
[End result customer wants] + [Specific time period] + [Address the objections]

Example 1:
[triple the conversions on your ecommerce store] + [in 3 days] + [or I'll refund your money]

Example 2:
[wipe away your debt] + [before your tax return is due] + [so the IRS won't call]

Or you can switch them around:
[I'll refund your money for this conference] + [if you don't get 7 real estate leads in one week]

The "Three Lenses" for headlines:

I always come up with a couple of different "angles" for headlines, and it's easy, because all I do is take the article I'm writing a headline for, and run it through these three lenses:

Competitive: This an aggressive headline that shows people "how to beat others".

"Download and steal all your competitors profitable keywords."

Benefit Driven: This simply shows the benefits of what your product/article/service does. Testimonials also work well here.

"Within 2 weeks you'll be playing your favorite Beatles song on the guitar!"

"I couldn't believe after only 2 weeks I was playing guitar at the Christmas party!"

Inspirational:

Shows that "even you" can do something. Paints a picture of the user getting some benefit from your product/service.

"You can teach your children to read by the age of 2 just by following these DVD's....all from your home."

Let's use the example of WPengine, a Wordpress hosting company.
Their current headline is: "Hassle free Wordpress hosting"

.....but now let's run it through our "three lenses":

Competitive:
"86% faster than regular Wordpress.....means more pageviews and better SEO"

Benefit Driven: (this one is simply using a testimonial):
"My site loads ridiculously fast, my pageviews are up, and my business is seeing the results!"

Inspirational:
"Even non-computer nerds can have a Wordpress site, with zero technical hassle"

Using those "lenses" as a framework will help you crank out completely different headlines quickly.

Aside from that, I try to make subject lines descriptive....and never "scammy"

If you send out regularly to a list of people, you can scam them into opening something like:

"Warning, change your info immediately"
-or-
"Why is there a squirrel in your yard??"

....yes, they will open silly subject lines at first, but they will feel betrayed once they find out you're just selling some crap to them.

Don't be scammy with your subject lines, it'll come back to you.

Keep your subject lines and headlines catchy and descriptive. Never scammy.

Ch. 10
Short vs. Long Copy

Ohhhh boy, this is a hot question I get:

"Is it better to write <u>short copy</u>, or <u>long copy</u>?"

I hear a lot of people saying long copy is ALWAYS better.
I then hear people who say SHORT forms are better for taking action.

In my experience I think it more depends on what you're selling.

If it's a difficult or expensive product, then longer is better.

If it's a simple and cheap product, then short is fine.

Let's imagine you're shopping online for something.....how much copy would it take to convince you to buy something?

If it's something simple and easy to sell? Like novelty yo-yo....
A picture of it and a short description like:

"3" diameter yo-yo is fun for ages 8 and up!"
Add to cart for $1.99

....might be all you need.

But what if we're selling something a little more complicated and expensive? In this case, it's gonna require a larger commitment on the buyers part (more money), so we might have
to do more convincing (longer copy) explaining the benefits.

For example, if we're trying to sell an expensive fan that costs over $350 like this Dyson Tower Fan, I would use more copy which sells more on emotion than specific details.

This is because if we're acting on strict specifications, it would be much more economical to buy a cheaper fan for less than $50 which can do the same thing (blow air). But THIS fan is not just a fan, so we need to convince people of that:

*

This is not a fan. It's a piece of art.

However it's also a fan.

Dyson created this bladeless work of art to be used as a conversation piece, work of art, and also a powerful fan unlike anything you've ever seen.

"Everyone who walks in my house first comments on the fan, and proceeds to put their hand through it in amazement wondering how it's blowing air. I can't believe how amazing it looks, and the conversations it starts!"
--Jenny C.

The fan draws in air from the base, and uses Air Multiplier technology to speed up the air 14x through a clever air-foil design.

You can run your fingers all over the fan, and even through it, with no possibility of injury since there are no moving parts to touch. This also makes this fan incredibly safe around children and pets.

Since the Dyson Tower Fan doesn't use blades, it blows air evenly like the wind outside. This means you can cool down a room with natural wind rather than a harsh fan. This effect must be experienced in person, as most people have never come in contact with a fan like this.

This innovation is only available through Dyson.

Dyson Tower Fan.
$350.00

So we used a little more copy to convince the buyer than with the yo-yo.

People already know what a basic yo-yo does, and writing more about it won't necessarily convince someone to buy it if they didn't already want it.

Here's the golden rule to remember:
Long copy is fine, so long as it's not **long-winded**.

Now if you can convince someone to take an action quickly, then fine. Imagine a signup for like this:

I will send you an email with a healthy breakfast recipe, every morning at 4am

This will help you eat better, have more energy,and hopefully lose some weight.

Just signup your email address here:

We can obviously add more copy explaining what people will be getting, but this basic outline pretty much covers most of it.

In this case, short copy was just fine, because it quickly communicated the idea across.

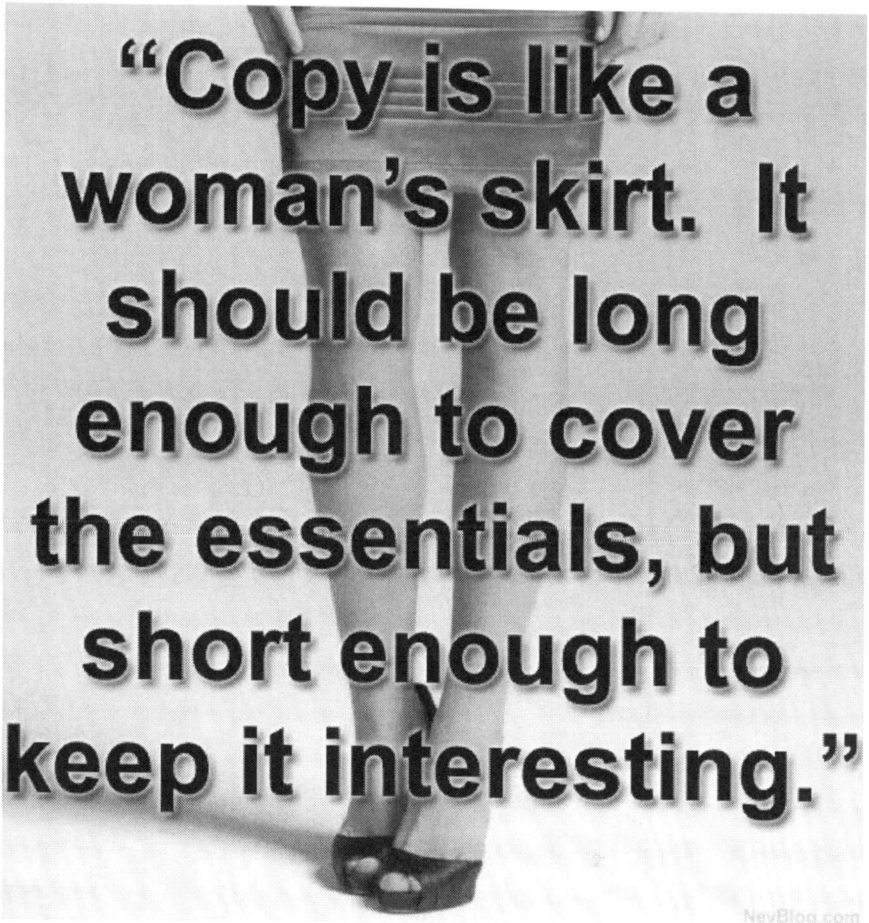
"Copy is like a woman's skirt. It should be long enough to cover the essentials, but short enough to keep it interesting."
NevBlog.com

Ch. 11
The Caveman Voice: Making things daaaaammmnn simple!

One of the biggest benefits I've had over other people who write, is that I'm DUMB!

That's right. My friend David always introduces me as "the smartest dumb guy I've ever met."

I simply can't grasp complex issues very easily. So I HAVE to break down complex ideas into smaller chunks to understand it myself.

So whenever I describe something to others, everyone understands, because it's broken down into such simple terms.

So when I'm reviewing copy, I have a VERY short attention span. If I lose the attention, or if some wording confuses me, I immediately try to go back and correct it, or delete it.

I started using a kind of "Caveman Voice" of grunts, such as:
- "ME NO LIKE!"
- "THIS MAKE NEVILLE BORED."
- "ME NO UNDERSTAND!"

This is a very silly, yet very helpful tactic for reviewing your own copy.

If at any point it lulls or bores you, **then it's gotta go.**

- Have a hilarious (yet obscure) Seinfeld joke? Don't use it. Don't make references only a small percentage of the audience will understand.

- Reading a paragraph and it's hard to read for some reason? Re-word it, or completely delete it. Is it even necessary?
- Are you TRYING to make something long, just for the sake of being long? If it's doing well short, then keep it short.

Another tactic to keeping something simple for a caveman is to use an easy analogy to explain a concept, like this:

> Nowadays with outsourcing being so easy, it's almost silly to spend months learning HTML to hand-code a website by yourself.....especially when you have more important things in your business to worry about. **That's like the CEO of WalMart wrangling carts from the parking lot himself, instead of paying someone else $8/hour to do it!**

Try to keep the amount of "brain cycles" it takes to communicate an idea....down to a minimum....and you'll keep your audiences attention much longer. Like this:

Question: What is 2 + 2?

Answer: 4

Easy enough. How about this one:

Question: What is the sum addition of a prime positive number that is the opposite of -2 and another number of the same qualities?

Answer: 4

You see how both answers were the same? Yet the second question made things WAAYYYY harder to understand.

This is an important principle of being a copywriter.
A good copywriter doesn't try to IMPRESS the reader......they try to INFORM the reader with the least amount of words.

This means not using fancy words when something can be said easier. For example:

Hard: "AppSumo is a company with vested interests to bring its consumers high quality discounts on useful software-as-a-service products for the digital age."

Easy: "This fat-ass Sumo sends you one MASSIVE money-saving deal on tech stuff for startups (like apps and software)... everyday."

Here's another example:
Hard: In an intriguing new development I have come to preclude in favor of the ruling of Senator Warren of his defense of Proposition 281-A of this jurisdictional adjourney governing velocity requirements on interstate highways.

Easy: We're putting Proposition 281-A into effect starting tomorrow. This means the speed limit is now 75 mph....Giddyup.

If you read something, and it requires "extra cycles" in your brain to process that information....scrap it. Get straight to the real point so everyone is CRYSTAL CLEAR on the message:

Hard: In this meeting we propose to infuse more symbiotic synergy between the Red Team and the Blue Team in lieu of recent events and transgressions over the past two weeks.

Easy: The Blue Team needs to apologize after you all pooped in the Red Team's shoes last week. Not cool guys. One more "pooping in shoes incident" and you're out of the race.

The only time you want to write something that is vague and confusing is if:
- You're a jerk trying to look cool by using confusing words.
- You're an evil lawyer trying to screw the other side with legal jargon.

As copywriters, we will chose to keep our message extraordinarily clear.

CH. 12
PRE-WRITING MENTAL CHECKLIST:

So you're at the end of this book, and you might be ready to to sit down and write. But lemme give you some advice from doing this thousands of times:

What your brain is thinking right now, is the way you're gonna write.

Feeling sad/tired/blue?
Your writing will probably come across as that.

Feeling fun/happy/playful?
Your writing will probably come across as that.

Feeling aggressive/intense?
Your writing will probably come across as that.

Here's some brain-hacks I use myself to get in the right state of mind.

CLEAN YOUR ROOM JOHNNY!
Try to clean your room or make your bed in one minute flat (pretend your new girlfriend just told you she's popping in, and you need to clean your room FAST).

SWEET SWEET DRUGS.
Drink some caffeine. This is a nice temporary solution. Red Bull, coffee or white tea is my fav. I've often had a beer when writing to switch my brain in a different mode (too much is counterproductive).

RINSE YOUR BRAIN.

Try a day where you eat exceedingly clean. Like all raw foods or smoothies for the first part of the day. If you're like me, you'll notice a huge increase in energy and brain activity.

STAY IN THE MOMENT, NO MATTER WHAT.

If writing inspirational stuff, then whenever you feel inspired, START WRITING AND DON'T STOP. I've jumped out of the shower just to write down inspired streams of thought.
If you're like me, there's maybe only 1-2 hours of really brilliant writing inside you each day.

WRITE FOR THE TONE YOU'RE IN:

Sometimes I'll wake up feeling crabby, and write an article in that not-taking-any-shit tone....and the feedback is TREMENDOUS because that pissed off mood helped me relate to something others are pissed about (example: Not being where they want to be in life).
Use those times when you're worried, sad, or angry to your advantage.

Now go out there and write some engaging and helpful copy!

CH. 13
:-(

Awww....I'm sad we're done with our time together :-(

Hopefully you picked up some tid-bits from this book that will stick with you forever. Even if it was one helpful trick, imagine how useful it'll be over your whole career.

Basically, if I impacted your life even just one little bit, I'll be happy.

HOWEVER, if that's not the case, then please feel free to get a full refund of this book. You can contact me here: NevBlog.com/contact

My pride and joy nowadays is the email list I send out most of my material to. You can signup up at NevBlog.com (you'll very obviously see the list there), or KopywritingKourse.com/hey

I send out 95% of what I write to that email list, and I've heard people tell me it's the ONLY newsletter they subscribe and take time to read. I think you'll enjoy it, and you and I can spend more time together :-)

Sincerely,
Neville Medhora

84182566R00031

Made in the USA
Lexington, KY
20 March 2018